The Story of S

written by Pam Bishop

illustrated by Beccy Blake, Chris Brown,
John Storey and Martin Ursell

Contents

What is scurvy?

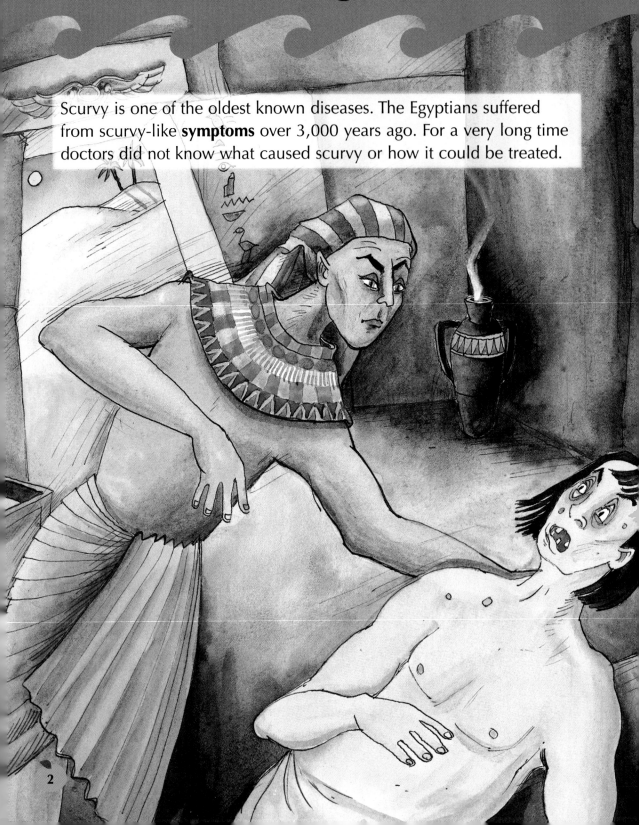

Scurvy is one of the oldest known diseases. The Egyptians suffered from scurvy-like **symptoms** over 3,000 years ago. For a very long time doctors did not know what caused scurvy or how it could be treated.

If you had the disease you were likely to die because you became very tired and could not walk or eat properly. Sores would appear in your mouth, your gums would bleed and your teeth would fall out. Your legs would bruise easily and become purple and swollen. The symptoms were very uncomfortable and very dangerous.

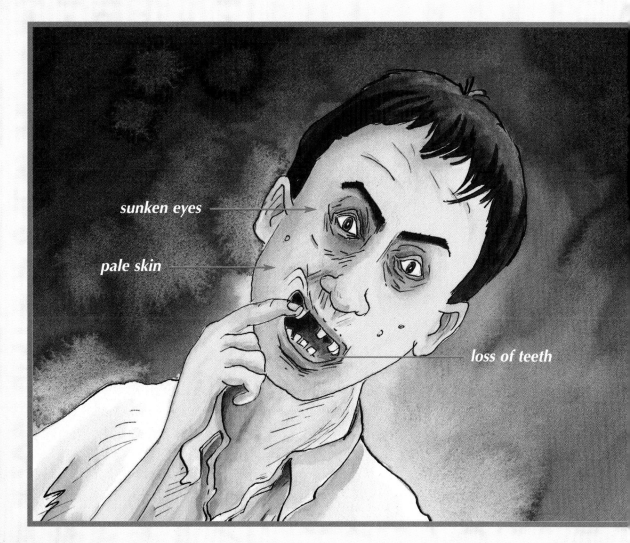

sunken eyes

pale skin

loss of teeth

Who suffered from scurvy?

In the 18th century scurvy was a very common disease amongst sailors.

At that time the British navy was the most powerful in the world. Its ships sailed all over the globe, travelling from India in the east to America in the west.

As the ships depended upon the wind to drive them along, sailors often spent many months at sea.

Vasco da Gama ▲

During their long voyages in sailing ships around the world, many sailors became ill and died of scurvy but nobody knew how to prevent or treat the illness.

On one trip made by the Portuguese **navigator**, Vasco da Gama, about 100 of his 170 crew died on board ship.

In 1593 Sir Richard Hawkins discovered that if his crew ate oranges and lemons they did not become ill. However, no one else made the connection between fruit and the prevention of scurvy until many years later.

Sir Richard Hawkins ▲

A clue to the disease

In the middle of the 18th Century a remarkable true story gave doctors a clue about the cause of the disease.

The story was about a particularly sick sailor. The sailor became so ill at sea and his legs were so swollen that he could not walk.

His captain was worried that the disease might affect the rest of his crew. He put the man ashore on a deserted island in the Atlantic and left him there to die.

However, to keep himself alive the sailor started to eat the fresh grass around him. Before long he was feeling better and started to move around again.

It seemed like a miracle, especially when the sailor got back to England on a passing ship and was able to tell his tale.

SAILOR SURVIVES SCURVY

Dr Lind's idea

A Scottish surgeon called Dr James Lind was very interested in this amazing story. He was a doctor in the navy and he knew how many sailors were dying of scurvy. He began to think about the problem. One idea he had was that scurvy was caused by a germ.

▲ *Dr Lind was interested in curing scurvy because he worked with many sailors who had died from the disease.*

However he thought that maybe there was a link between scurvy and the grass that the sailor had eaten on the island.

He thought that perhaps scurvy had something to do with the food that the sailors were eating. This was his **hypothesis**.

Dr Lind's experiment

On 20 May 1747 Dr Lind began an experiment at sea with twelve sick sailors on board a ship called the *Salisbury*. They had all been well looked after with plenty of food – meat broth, porridge, biscuits, rice, raisins and currants, all washed down with wine. However, after a couple of months, they had the symptoms of scurvy and were not fit to carry out their duties.

Dr Lind divided the men into six pairs. They all had their normal diet but in addition he gave a different treatment to each of the six groups.

- Group 1 drank a mug of cider each day

- Group 2 gargled with very mild sulphuric acid

- Group 3 had two spoonfuls of vinegar, three times each day

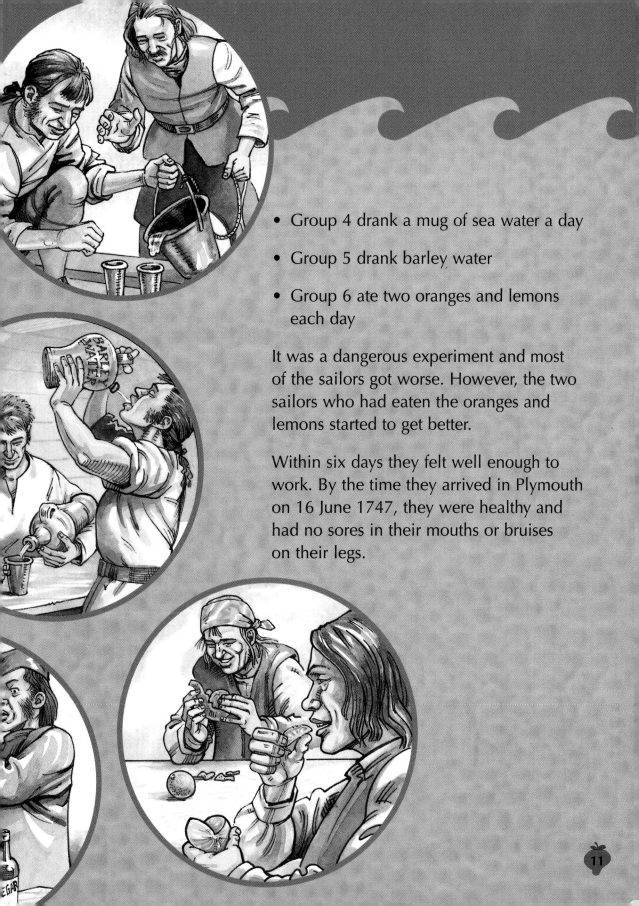

- Group 4 drank a mug of sea water a day

- Group 5 drank barley water

- Group 6 ate two oranges and lemons each day

It was a dangerous experiment and most of the sailors got worse. However, the two sailors who had eaten the oranges and lemons started to get better.

Within six days they felt well enough to work. By the time they arrived in Plymouth on 16 June 1747, they were healthy and had no sores in their mouths or bruises on their legs.

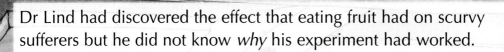

Dr Lind had discovered the effect that eating fruit had on scurvy sufferers but he did not know *why* his experiment had worked.

How had the fruit managed to cure the men? Did **acid** in the fruit kill off the disease or was it something else in the oranges and lemons? How did the fruit have the same effect as the fresh grass that the sailor on the island had eaten?

It was still a mystery. When sailors began their voyages they usually took fresh fruit and vegetables on board but had to eat them up quickly before they became old and rotten. The crew of some ships also drank lemon juice but they boiled it first to keep it fit for drinking throughout their long journey. These changes in diet helped, but sailors continued to get ill from scurvy.

Dr Lind's experiment did help to save the lives of many sailors. However, some sailors still suffered from scurvy and the reasons for this were not discovered for over 150 years.

In fact Dr Lind continued to work on his ideas for about another forty years. In 1794 the navy allowed him to carry out another experiment. A whole fleet of ships was supplied with enough raw lemon juice to last for a six month voyage. Not one sailor suffered from scurvy during that time.

Doctors still thought that the important ingredient was the acid in the fruit. Since lime juice contains even more acid they decided that this would work better.

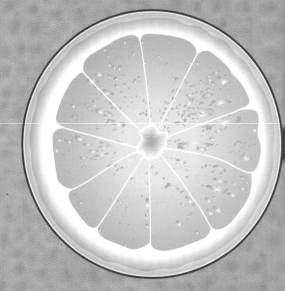

In 1795, the British navy made it compulsory for all sailors to have fresh lime juice in their diet whilst at sea. It had the right effect. Scurvy was no longer a problem.

Today conditions in the navy are very different but British sailors are still sometimes nicknamed "limeys".

A lime a day keeps the scurvy away!

What causes disease?

In the nineteenth century doctors slowly started to understand what caused different illnesses and how they could be treated.

Doctors and scientists carried out many experiments on how to

protect people from getting killer diseases like **smallpox**

treat people with **cholera**

carry out surgical operations safely and stop germs getting into wounds

prevent diseases spreading by keeping air and water supplies clean and fresh.

▲ *In 1796 Dr Jenner developed a vaccination to prevent people from getting smallpox.*

◀ *In 1854 John Snow proved that the spread of cholera was linked to dirty water supplies.*

16

◀ *Joseph Lister carried out a knee operation using an antiseptic to stop infection of the wound.*

But most people still thought that it was the acid in the fresh fruit that killed off germs and cured scurvy.

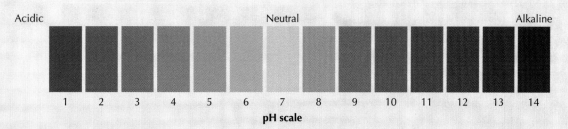

Acidic   Neutral   Alkaline

1   2   3   4   5   6   7   8   9   10   11   12   13   14

pH scale

▲ *Acidity is measured by its pH value.*

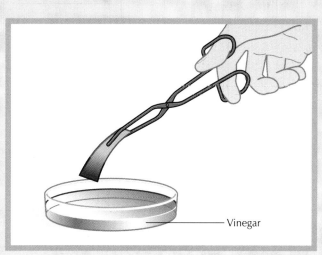

Vinegar

Indicator paper ▶ changes colour to show the pH of a liquid.

The discovery of vitamins

It was not until the beginning of the 20th century that scientists unlocked the secret. Dr Lind had in fact discovered the power of **vitamins** even though vitamins were not known about until 1911.

The Daily News

VITAMINS DISCOVERED!

The News Today

FINALLY, THE TRUTH IS OUT!

Dr Lind's experiment in 1747 was the beginning of the search for vitamins.

Scientists all over the world were researching different diseases and made important discoveries, often by accident.

For example, scientists found that although animals like mice were being well fed, they became ill if important chemicals were missing from their **diet**. These chemicals were not needed in large amounts. They did not supply the animals with energy to live and grow, but they did keep them healthy and fit.

These essential chemicals were called vitamins.

Scientists continue their work in hospitals today to find new cures for diseases.

Vitamin C

The vitamin responsible for preventing scurvy was not found until the 1930s.

Scientists carried out experiments with lemon juice to try to track down the important chemical. Finally they managed to make a liquid from the lemons that was 20,000 times stronger than the lemon juice itself. They analysed this liquid to work out exactly what it was made of. Finally they had discovered vitamin C! (Its proper chemical name is **ascorbic acid**.)

Today we can get vitamin C by eating fruit and vegetables or by taking vitamin C pills.

This vitamin can now be made and bought in bottles so that everybody can get as much vitamin C as they need, even if they do not eat enough of the right foods.

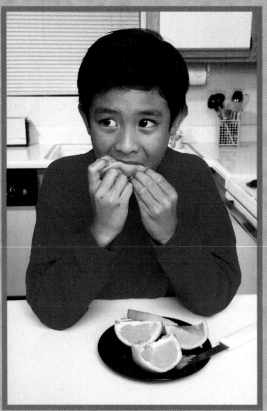

The scientists had found an explanation for the work that Dr Lind had done almost 200 years earlier. They also proved that illness is not always caused by infection from an attack of germs.

It is sometimes caused by a **deficiency**, or something missing in the diet. Scurvy is a **deficiency disease** caused by a lack of vitamin C in what people eat.

▲ *A balanced diet helps to prevent deficiency diseases.*

A healthy diet

The very best foods
for providing vitamin
C in our diet are fresh
fruit and vegetables.

Citrus fruits such as oranges, lemons,
grapefruit and tangerines contain high levels of the
vitamin. So do blackcurrants, melons, kiwi and
strawberries and vegetables like green and red peppers,
tomatoes, potatoes, cabbage and broccoli.

Green grass is also useful – as the sailor on
the island found out! But there are
more enjoyable ways of getting the
right amount of vitamin C.

Doctors now tell us that we
should eat at least five servings
of fruit or vegetables every day
and the story about the discovery
of vitamins explains why. `

But ... why didn't boiled lemon juice stop sailors from getting scurvy?

Cooking food for too long and at too high a temperature destroys the vitamins. If fruit and vegetables are boiled the vitamin C escapes into the cooking water and is usually thrown away. Fruit and vegetables also lose most of their vitamins if they are left to get old or if they are cut open and not eaten straight away.

So, fresh fruit and vegetables are good for health. Most of them taste very good, too!

What does vitamin C do?

What does vitamin C do in the body to help prevent scurvy?

Vitamin C is important for maintaining healthy bones. Without vitamin C the skeleton would not be strong. Arms and legs that are broken would be slow to mend.

Vitamin C also prevents the body from catching other diseases and helps to fight off infections. So it is not surprising that the sailors, who went on long voyages without fruit and vegetables, became weak and ill.

Vitamin C maintains healthy teeth and gums.

Vitamin C is needed for making **collagen** in the body. Collagen is essential for keeping bones, tendons and ligaments strong.

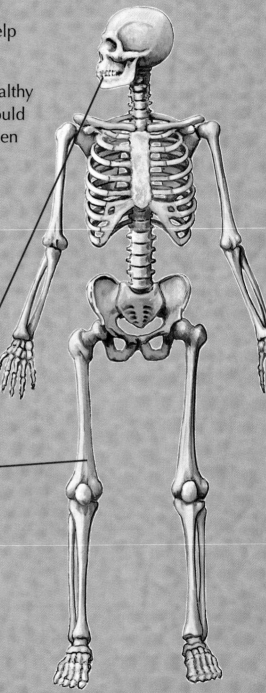

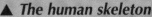
▲ *The human skeleton*

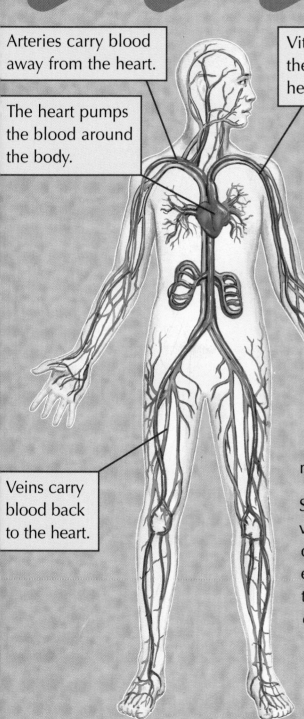

Arteries carry blood away from the heart.

The heart pumps the blood around the body.

Vitamin C is carried around the body in the blood, through veins and arteries. It helps the body to heal cuts and bruises.

Veins carry blood back to the heart.

▲ *The circulatory system*

But ... why didn't the fresh fruit they ate at the start of the voyage stop sailors getting scurvy?

Vitamin C is carried around in the blood. Once the body has taken what it needs the rest cannot be stored. It is passed out in urine when we go to the toilet. That is why it is important to eat foods rich in vitamin C every day and not just once in a while.

Some people believe that if you take extra vitamins you can avoid getting some serious diseases. But scientists do not yet know enough about the effects on the body of taking high levels of vitamins (sometimes called 'mega-dosing'). In fact very high levels of vitamin C may damage your stomach and kidneys. It is probably best to stick with a good healthy diet.

Scurvy today

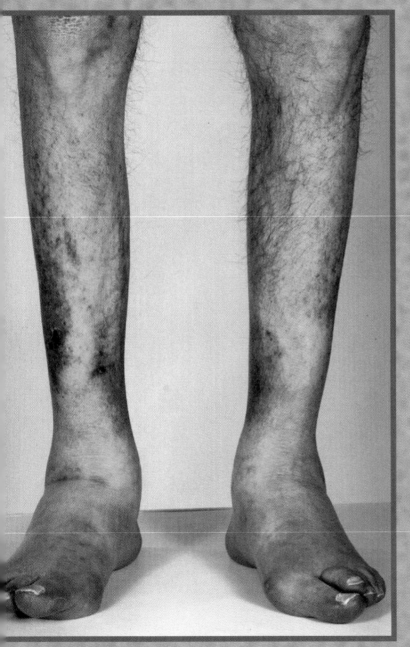

You may think that scurvy is a disease of the past, or that it is found only in parts of the world where people do not have the chance to eat a proper balanced diet every day.

Today, babies and old people may still suffer from scurvy, although it is not common. Scurvy in the very young is called *Barlow's disease*. It can occur if babies are not given enough fruit juice to drink when they stop having milk from their mother.

▲ *The bruised and swollen legs of a scurvy sufferer.*

Scientists in the USA found that three per cent of students in one university had low levels of vitamin C in their blood. A bigger survey across America showed that over seven million American adults are in danger of getting scurvy.

Doctors have worked out how much vitamin C we should take every day. Men should have more than women. Women who are having babies need extra. About forty per cent of men and women do not take the amount recommended and could become ill with scurvy symptoms.

It is important not to worry about getting scurvy. Dr James Lind and other doctors have proved that if we eat enough fruit and vegetables we will not suffer from scurvy.

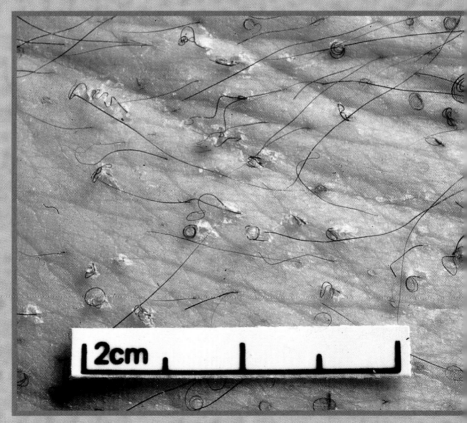

▲ *Corkscrew hairs on the skin of a patient suffering from scurvy.*

Timeline

1700s
Many sailors on long sea
voyages died of scurvy

1795
The British navy said
that lime juice must be
carried on all ships

1747
Dr James Lind carried
out an experiment on
twelve sailors

1800s
Many scientific
advances were made
the field of medicir

1935
Vitamin C was the first pure vitamin to be produced and sold to the public

1911
Vitamins were discovered

1931
Ascorbic acid (vitamin C) was identified in lemon juice

The News Today

FINALLY, THE TRUTH IS OUT!

Dr Lind's experiment in 1747 was the beginning of the search for vitamins.

Glossary

acid   a sour liquid

ascorbic acid   the chemical name for vitamin C

cholera   a very serious disease carried in dirty water or food. The patient is very sick and has diarrhoea

collagen   a protein found in skin, bone, cartilage and tendon which acts as a glue, holding the body together

diet   all the foods that we eat

deficiency   lack or shortage

deficiency disease   an illness caused by a lack of something in the diet

hypothesis   an idea used as the starting point for
planning an experiment

navigator   sailor and explorer

symptom   a sign or feature of disease

smallpox   a very serious disease spread by the air or
by touching someone who has the disease already.
The patient has red spots full of pus.

vitamins   substances needed in small amounts in the
diet to stay healthy. They are called vitamin A, B, C,
D, E, K and M

Index